PENNY THE PITTIE

Journey to Freedom

Written by: Sherry L. Samples

Illustrated by: Mariia Luzina

Mali Pas Creative, LLC books may be purchased for educational, business, or sales promotional use. Special editions including signed copies may be made available upon request.

For details, contact MaliPasCreative@yahoo.com / subject line: Special Editions

First Printing, 2024

Published by Mali Pas Creative, LLC

ISBN: 979-8-9904160-0-0

In memory of Beau

&

The special people who loved and cared for him.

Emily Gaugh, DVM

Kimberly Gugler, DVM

Heather Heeb, DVM DACVIM (Oncology)

Marie Mahn, RVT

David Senter, DVM DACVD

Out in the countryside far away, there lived a special dog named Penny the Pittie. Penny lived in a muddy yard, surrounded by her family, which included 60 brothers, sisters, cousins, aunts, uncles, grandma, grandpa, and even a flock of chickens. You see, Penny's family had started with just two dogs three years ago, and they had grown into a big, loving bunch that was being hoarded by a man and a woman.

But even though Penny the Pittie was never alone and had lots of family members, her life was not a happy one. In winter, she shivered from the cold, in summer, she sweated from the heat, and when it rained, she was always covered in mud because she didn't have a cozy house like the chickens did. Penny wondered, "Why don't *I* have a home like the chickens?"

Penny the Pittie never got to have a bath, her nails were so long that her feet hurt, and no one ever told her she was pretty or loved. The people who took care of Penny's family wouldn't let them out to play and kept them in a tiny, uncomfortable space with sharp barbed wire, metal, and glass.

Penny the Pittie's tummy often rumbled with hunger, as there was never enough food. Every day, the people would toss just one bag of garbage in the yard. If Penny wanted to eat, she had to compete with her family as they tore the bag apart, hoping for something they could eat. Penny the Pittie was very thin.

People who came to see Penny the Pittie and her family feared them. Parents wouldn't let their children play with Penny and her family. Parents said those dogs were "dangerous" and "mean."

Penny and her family were special dogs called Pitties or Pit Bulls, but many people thought they were bad and not to be trusted, even though long ago they were considered very special by kings and queens who trusted them to watch over their children. Penny the Pittie couldn't understand why they were so feared.

They had never hurt anyone.

At night, Penny the Pittie dreamed of a better life. She dreamed of walking on the beautiful green grass she saw on the neighbor's farm and of people not being afraid of her.

One day some ladies came to visit Penny the Pittie's family and the people who kept them. When they left, they took some of Penny's family with them. Penny the Pittie looked on sadly.

Two days later, more people came back and brought a big bag that smelled so good. Penny the Pittie's family ran and began clawing at the bag. Penny had never had dog food in her less than two years. When they left, they took more of Penny's family members but left poor little Penny the Pittie.

One week passed with more ladies coming and taking some more of Penny the Pittie's family members. This time Penny knew that she had to get their attention, so she pushed her way to the front of the fence, cut her tummy on the barbed wire and began barking and yelping as if to say, "Pick me." One of the ladies, Yara, looked at Penny the Pittie and said, "Oh, she is so pretty." Penny's body was twisting and her tail wagging as she heard this. She thought surely the lady would take her away.

The lady came in and picked up some of Penny the Pittie's siblings, put them in a box with a handle, and took them to her car. Penny awaited her return, but it was not to be. Penny the Pittie was so sad. She was left behind again. She held her mud-covered head down over the barbed wire fence as the ladies drove away.

More weeks passed, and Penny the Pittie lost all hope for a better life.
Only Penny and three of her siblings remained.

Then, one day, Yara came and remembered Penny. She leaned over the fence, rubbed her head, and smiled as she handed Penny a treat. It was a strange experience because Penny had never had a treat before.

The lady stepped over the fence, put Penny in a strange-looking container, and closed the door.
Penny the Pittie was scared, trembling, whimpering, and crying as she was carried to a car. Where was the lady taking her?

As the car journeyed through the countryside and into the city, Penny the Pittie was filled with anxiety. In the car, Yara comforted Penny, saying, "There's no need to be scared, Penny. I've come to rescue you and take you to a better place."

When they arrived at a big building, Yara placed Penny the Pittie's container on the floor. It was a hot day and the cool building felt so good to Penny. Inside, Penny the Pittie saw beautiful clean dogs of all colors and sizes that looked just like her. They rushed to greet her, and Yara said, "Penny, you now have a safe place to stay, plenty of food every day, and all the love you could ever want."

As Yara let Penny the Pittie out of her container she saw other people hugging the dogs and others wanting to hug her.
With newfound friends who loved her no matter what and did not fear her.

Penny the Pittie finally knew what it was like to be a dog and to be safe at the rescue shelter. She finally knew what it felt like to be happy.

Final Thoughts

Thank you for reading the true story of Pennie the Pittie. Although Penny's outcome appears to be a happy one because she makes it to a wonderful rescue shelter, not all dogs are so lucky. Thousands of dogs end up in shelters every day, and a great percentage are Pit Bulls or Pit Bull mixes often lovingly referred to as Pitties. However, you can make a difference. Check out the local shelters and rescues in your area. You can volunteer to take dogs for a walk, visit the dogs, and in some locations take a dog for a "Dog's Day Out" to allow them time to decompress from the stress of a shelter. These events may be done as a family depending on the rules of the shelter or rescue. You can donate money, food, treats, blankets, or toys. Or maybe...you can foster or adopt a Penny the Pittie of your own.

Happy Tails

www.ingramcontent.com/pod-product-compliance
Lightning Source LLC
Chambersburg PA
CBHW041501120626
46547CB00003B/500